Introduction

I own several books on Sheffield industries - mostly well illustrate  ...ures - often showing processes and workmen at their various tasks. They depict the history of our industrial city at work. What I have had more difficulty in finding is information on the location of the buildings that were so well-known to our older citizens - Cyclops Works, River Don Works, Tinsley Rolling Mills, Davy United, Brown Bayleys etc.

So what I have tried to do in this book is to show the works as I photographed them with information of where I was at the time. What I am aiming at is a geography of Sheffield industry rather than another history.

Most of these photos were taken in the 1970s or early 1980s when the great firms were already in decline. I wish I had taken them earlier but, alas, it is too late now. Many of the building have been demolished. Some have been converted to other uses. Fortuantely I did rather go mad and ran through hundreds of feet of negative film so that what I have picked out is only a selection.

In my five previous book I have tried to capture something of our vanishing city, here I am having another go.

I would also like to thank all the people who have written to me about my previous efforts.

The Cutlass Works on Sidney Street were photographed in 1977.

This view of industrial Brightside dates from around 1976 and belies its name. It was taken from somewhere near to Hawkshead Road.

Looking down Old Hall Road in Attercliffe gives a glimpse of the massive Brown Bayley works as they looked in 1965. The Golden Ball pub on the left was later re-named The Turnpike before it was finally demolished to make way for the Stadium.

CAMMELLS STEEL WORKS, SHEFFIELD.

The Cammell Laird Cyclops works were located at the junction of Newhall Road and Carlisle Street East. This photograph dates from before the First World War.

This was taken at Attercliffe, Coleridge Road, in the 1960s. I believe the works were part of the Brown Bayley empire.

These two public houses, Fitzwilliam and Wentworth, on Milford Street stand in the shadow of the English Steel works viewed from Attercliffe Common on 12th June 1983. The works are now adorned by the Forgemasters logo.

This is a view of the tow-path of the Sheffield Canal taken from Bacon Lane bridge, looking toward Sheffield city centre.

Bacon Lane Bridge over the Sheffield Canal is one of the original 1819 canal bridges and was notoriously difficult to navigate. The date was 17th May 1974.

Industrial Attercliffe - where Attercliffe Road crosses the River Don.
Taken from Effingham Road or Stoke Street on 17th May 1974.

The River Don at Hawke Street showing the works bordering the river taken on 12th June 1983.

Tinsley Rolling Mills were situated on a strip of land between Sheffield Canal and the River Don. All of it has now disappeared.

The Sheffield Simplex motor works were at Tinsley in the days when we actually made motors in Sheffield. They were situated on Sheffield Road at the corner of Lock Lane and are clearly shown on the 1921 OS map.

A scene to make the mouth of any motor cycle enthusiast water. This shop and repair centre was at the bottom of Ecclesall Road around 1925. Notice the motor-bike and sidecar parked outside. When did you last see one of those?

A view of Meadow Hall in 1976. The photograph shows both the railway viaduct and the Tinsley viaduct. Meadow Bank Road is the road in the distance. Many historians believe that the great Battle of Brunanburh, 937AD, was fought on this site

Taken from Tinsley Viaduct walkway on the Rotherham side, in 1977.

Another view of Meadow Hall and the Tinsley viaduct in 1977. Here we are looking south. Ironically this was called Blackburn Meadows

This is Brown Bayley's Rotherham Works at Tinsley, taken in 1977.

The left side of Blonk Street was largely part of the Samuel Osborne Empire.
In the distance can be seen the Canal Basin.
The date of the photograph was 1976.

Samuel Osborne's Clyde Steel Works as seen from above Blonk Street bridge. The date was 1974.

Above:
A Whitbread tanker and crew.
Samuel Whitbread started a brewery in 1742.

Left:
The Exchange brewery on Bridge Street with steam up here viewed from Lady's Bridge.

Both these photographs were taken in 1976.

The Exchange Brewery occupied much of the north side of Bridge Street. Now there is just an entrance gate and beyond it yet another block of nondescript flats with a gate-man to keep out the non-residents.

The industrial River Don viewed from Lady's Bridge as it was in 1976.
The view is very different today and they tell me the river is cleaner.

This is a photograph of Bridgehouses in the 1930s. The notice reads London & North Eastern Bridghouses Goods Depot. Farther to the right is the Manchester Hotel pub and then the huge Aizlewood mill.
The 18th century iron footbridge in the foreground still stands, but for how much longe?

Bridgehouses Station approach is a magnificent example of Victorian building.
Alas, now it is closed off so this view of our lost industries would not now be possible.
The chimney and surround works were Sheffield Forge Mills.
This photograph dates from 1975.

Townhead Street showing the external appearance
of the yard shown in the following picture.
The date is the 18th July 1974.

This works entrance was at 53 Townhead Road. F. J. Harding & Co. were boot and shoe manufacturers while sharing the same yard was Henry Willis and Son Ltd - organ builders of international repute.

Looking up Townhead Street - again on the 18th July 1974. On the right is the important firm of Needham Engineering - wholesale suppliers of tools, electrical goods, radios and televisions etc. Sitting on the wall was a lady whose bags are full of food for Sheffield's pigeons.

W & J.A. Baxter Ltd. occupied Congo Works at 30 Trippet Lane. The 1973 Directory - the same date as this photograph - describes them as cutlery manufacturers. Samuel Woodcock and Sons Ltd shared the same building.

At the time of writing the future of the Anglo Works at the corner of Trippet Lane and Holly Lane is in some doubt. This photograph was taken in August 1970 when the works were still producing "spoons, forks and E.P. cutlery".

Eyre Lane near Charles Street shown as it was in 1965 with a host of little mesters' premises. The lane still exists but looks very different.

A chair factory in Hawley Croft in 1898.

Brightside Lane shortly before the entrance to Firth Brown's and Firth Vickers was closed for ever.
The date was 30th July 1983.

The taxi and motor cyclist are waiting on Bedford Street to enter Rutland Road. This was once the short-cut to Pitsmoor. On the right are Bury's Regent Works. The date was May 1977.

These Truro Works are situated on Matilda Street where it meets Shoreham Street. When I took this on 13th July 1974 they belonged to Irving White Ltd., makers of engineering tools and equipment. They have now been tarted up and made into flats. On the extreme right of the picture is a "public convenience". Since they have virtually disappeared from our streets it has historic interest.

Broad Lane at Red Hill as it was in 1978.
The historic Montgomery drinking fountain (not shown) was to the left of the photograph.

This view of the massive Joseph Rodgers & Sons works that bordered the River Sheaf was taken from above the Midland Station in 1975. They were manufacturers of all kinds of knives, scissors, razors, spoons and forks as well as silver and electro-plate. See the next page for an interior view. All has now gone for ever.

River Lane entrance to Joseph Rodgers works.
8th May 1984.

This view is looking towards the River Lane
entrance opposite. The date is the same.

Marsh Brothers occupied Ponds Steel Works on Shude Lane for three Centuries before they were demolished to make way for Ponds Forge swimming baths. Sydney Pollard wrote a book about these works entitled "Three Centuries of Sheffield Steel".

Arundel Street as it looked in 1977.
The works are those of Cooper Brothers
at the Don Plate Works.
They were well-known for their
"Staybrite" cutlery as well as
pewter and electro-plated goods.

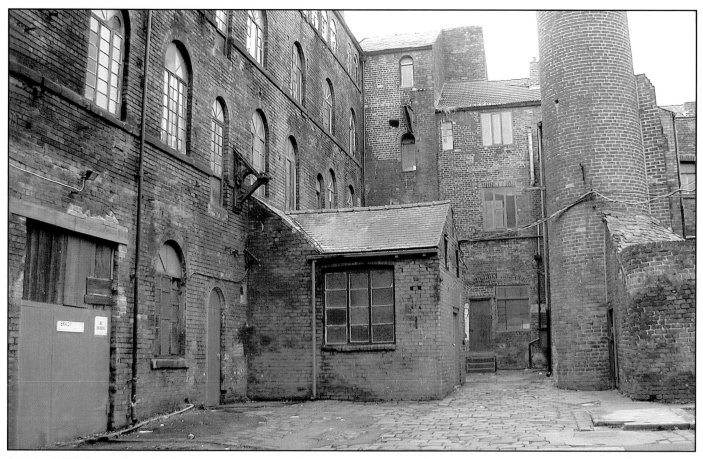

Butcher's Works on Arundel Street is one of the few remaining and unchanged examples in the city. An ideal location for any TV serial on Northern industry in Victorian times.

Trafalgar Street is here seen from Division Street.
There were many works situated here.

Trafalgar Street in 1985 showing the yard of one of the works.

This view over the River Don at Nursery Street shows the Millsands Works that have been demolished and replaced with a large expanse of expensive flats.
The Don has now become a very pleasant waterside feature.
This is how it looked in 1982.

The Spartan Works manufactured Stainless Steel
and they were situated on Attercliffe Road.
The photograph was taken in 1985.

Carter & Co. were manufacturing chemists famous for "Carter's Little Liver Pills". They were on Attercliffe Road near Washford bridge.

Countess Road looking towards Bramall Lane football ground. The date is 1980 when Sheffield men were still using safety razors and Wardonia blades led the rest.

George Butler, Cutler's Works, were situated where Sidney Street runs into Matilda Street. A new and rather boring modern building has replaced them. The date of the photograph was 1983.

This is West Street at Bailey Lane some 25 years ago showing the Morton Block of little mester workshops before they were ripped to pieces with only the frontage retained. Morton's scissor shop provided the retail outlet. The old Saddle pub is on the right.

This is No. 53 Gell Street in 1977. Home of the cutlery works of William Bocking. They were manufacturers of table knives established in 1838.

This unique photograph was taken from the Royal Hospital looking over Orange Street towards three cementation chimneys. The firm of C.F. Johnson on the right manufactured tools. The date was around 1938.

Here at the Neepsend end of Rutland Road bridge is a view of Samuel Osborne's works on the other side of the River Don. The date was 16th June 1974.

Wostenholme's Washington Works is viewed from Eldon Street. George Wosteholme and Son Ltd. were cutlery manufacturers. These impressive works were on Wellington Street but are now gone. Date was 26th July 1974.

Carver Street above Division Street. At the date of this photograph (1972) the white building (No. 23) housed a variety of small businesses from cutlery and scissor manufacturers to model railway enthusiasts. Kelly's 1970 Directory gives full details.

Carver Lane is to be found above the City Hall.The cars are parked in Holly Street car park but the buildings were on Carver Lane and have now been demolished. They typify the small industrial premises that were a feature of much of central Sheffield before they began to disappear following the decline of British manufacturing industry.
The date of the photograph is 1972.

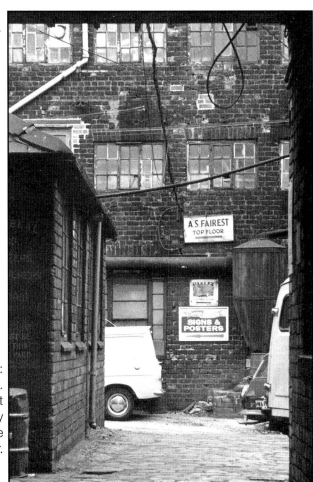

Left:
No. 19 Carver Street. Globe Works. George Herrett. pewter manufacturer. Taken in 1973.
See page 54.

Right:
23 Carver St. A.S. Fairest was a cutlery maker on the top floor.

A lot of industry was to be found near Ecclesall Road. Edward Pryor & Son's works were on Broom Street. The photograph was taken on 18th July 1974.

This is Headford Street where Milton Street crosses it. The main building is Milton Works which my 1970 directory informs me was in use by H. Rowbotham & Co. Ltd, cutlery manufacturers.
The date of the photograph was 1976.

The Kutrite Works were here on Snow Lane when this was taken in 1983. Now they have relocated at the corner of Russell Street.
This area is in danger of disappearing when the new ring road is built.

This is Bowling Green Street on the 8th May 1974. The road running to the left is South Parade. Beyond South Parade Spear and Jackson's (Ashberry) Ltd. were in occupation. On the left is Arthur Mudford's - manufacturers of tarpaulin.

Looking down Green Lane towards Penistone Road. We have the imposing entrance to the Globe Works to our right and to the left is the Don Brewery. Between them can be seen the graveyard of St. Philip's church and beyond is Infirmary Road. The name plate from the brewery has been retained and built into the refurbished area. The date is 1976.

Malinda St. looking towards the Infirmary.
Left are the works of Austin McGillivray,
file and steel makers.
The year is 1973.

Alma Street May 1974.
The splendid Britannia Mills fill the picture.
On a recent visit all this has now
disappeared.

Lambert St. John Watts established 1765. Photographed in 1984. These are historic buildings. I was fortunate to be able to take my picture when there was empty space available. For more information about these works see an article by Peter Machan in "Aspects of Sheffield 2", Wharncliffe Publishing 1999.

This was how Penistone Road looked in May 1983. To the right was Bedford Street and to the left Rutland Road.
The Regent Works are on the left of the picture.

The River Don at Penistone Road showing the Toledo Steelworks on the opposite bank. The photograph dates from 1968.

On Penistone Road, Osborne's Mushet Tools building is a landmark. The little works by its side are dwarfed by their imposing neighbour.
The photograph dates from 1975.

Left:
This is the entrance to Bury's Regent Works. The date was 1983.

Right:
A shot of Abbeydale Industrial Works as they were in the 1950s.

Pearson's Forge on Penistone Road on a cold winter's day in 1975 billowing steam over Owlerton Bridge.

This is an old photograph of the Stocksbridge Works as they were around 1910.

STOCKBRIDGE

A cluster of works in the Claywheels area. The now demolished
Wadsley Bridge School can be seen bottom right.
The date was 5th June 1983.

These works have now gone and a housing estate has been built on the site. Sheffield University carried out a dig before all traces were finally obliterated.

DENTON'S FORGE. WISEWOOD. 176.

FURNISS, SHEFFIELD.

These works in the Loxley Valley belonged to Marshall's. Here photographed fully active in 1977.

This view of the Sheffield to Tinsley Canal from 1977 gives a good view of the Sheaf Works when Thomas Turton & Sons, steel manufacturers, were in occupation. It was latterly converted into a public house when the whole area was revamped.

Smithy Wood Coking Plant stood above Chapeltown and the pollution caused a lot of aggravation.
With the collapse of the mining industry it has now gone forever. The date was around the middle 1970s.

T.W. Ward's Albion Works fronted on Savile Street. This view was taken from Effingham Road showing the back of them. The imposing frontage can still be seen but the interior may have gone. This dates from 1980.

Here are works at the junction of Granville Street and South Street. They are now somewhere under the huge Park Square - though how a circle can be called a square I do not know. Various firms occupied the premises. Dated 28th August 1965.

Sheffield Canal Basin back in 1974
when it was still busy working
and not just for pleasure cruising

A view of industrial Neepsend from 1963.

Mary Street is to be found near Ecclesall Road. In 1975 when this photograph was taken it was heavily industrial.